ED

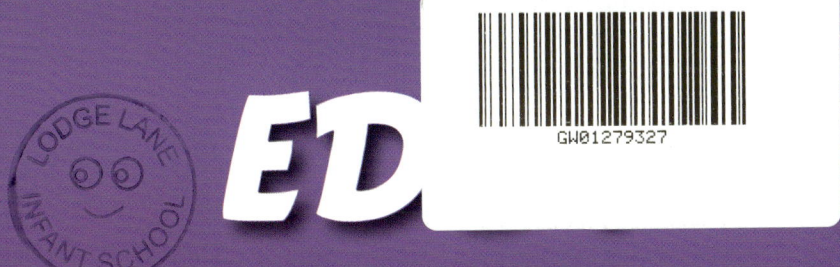

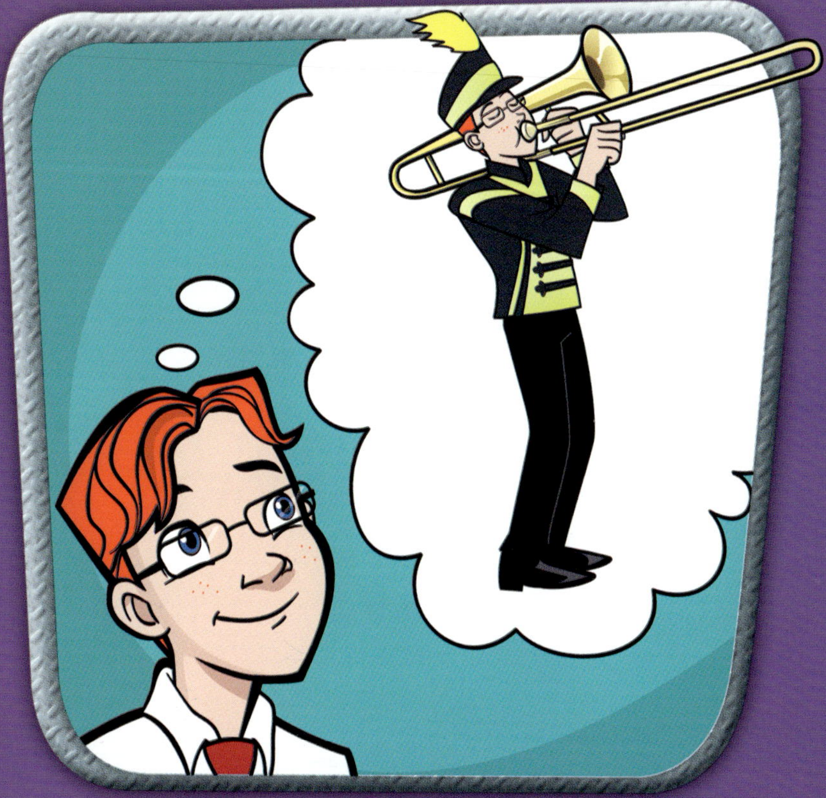

Written by Monica Hughes
Illustrated by James Elston

Eddy had a new trombone and a new music teacher!

She showed him the way to hold a trombone and rest the tube on his shoulder.

She told Eddy to continue playing the trombone every day. Then he might get into the school band.

Eddy tried to play at home. But it was hard pushing the tube to and fro.

Eddy's family did not help! It amused his brother to use the trombone to poke Mum.

Then Eddy tried to use his sister's scarf to polish the trombone.

She refused to let him have it, and called him a pest.

Only Grandad was kind. He said, "Eddy, you are like me when I was a lad."

He let Eddy play the trombone at his house.

Eddy liked using Grandad's attic. He went round every day and slowly Eddy got better at playing the trombone.

At last Eddy's music teacher told him he could join the band. And so he got his gold tunic.

Eddy's family went wild when they spied him in the band.

"Hooray!" they cried proudly.

After that, Eddy played his trombone at home and everyone liked the lively music!